XTREME SCREAMS

THE WORLD'S MOST GHOULISH
Ghosts

A&D Xtreme
BOLD HI-LO NONFICTION

An imprint of Abdo Publishing
abdobooks.com

S.L. HAMILTON

TAKE IT TO
THE XTREME!

GET READY FOR AN XTREME ADVENTURE! THE PAGES OF THIS BOOK WILL TAKE YOU INTO THE THRILLING WORLD OF THE MOST GHOULISH GHOSTS ON EARTH. WHEN YOU HAVE FINISHED READING THIS BOOK, TAKE THE XTREME CHALLENGE ON PAGE 45 ABOUT WHAT YOU'VE LEARNED!

ABDOBOOKS.COM

Published by Abdo Publishing, a division of ABDO, PO Box 398166, Minneapolis, Minnesota 55439. Copyright © 2022 by Abdo Consulting Group, Inc. International copyrights reserved in all countries. No part of this book may be reproduced in any form without written permission from the publisher. A&D Xtreme™ is a trademark and logo of Abdo Publishing.

Printed in the United States of America, North Mankato, MN.
032021
092021

THIS BOOK CONTAINS
RECYCLED MATERIALS

Editor: John Hamilton; Copy Editor: Bridget O'Brien
Graphic Design: Sue Hamilton
Cover Design: Laura Graphenteen   Cover Photo: iStock
Interior Photos & Illustrations: Alamy-pgs 6-7 & 8-9; Antix Productions-pg 41 (bottom); AP-pgs 24 (Marcianos), 29 & 34-35; Chip Coffey-pg 17 (middle); Columbia Pictures-pg 40 (middle); Find-a-Grave-pgs 24 (gravestone) & 25 (cemetery); Getty-pgs 9 (wounded), 16 & 28 (plane); Harvey Comics-pg 39 (Casper); iStock-pgs 1 (ghost), 19 & 25 (woman); James Randi-pg 17 (bottom); John Edward-pg 17 (top); Keene State College-pg 22; Marvel Comics-pg 39 (bottom left); Namco-pg 42 (top); NASA-pg 1 (Moon); NBC Universal-pg 41 (top); Nintendo-pg 42 (middle & bottom); Queen Mary-pg 27 (top inset); Shutterstock-pgs 4-5, 10-11, 20-21; 22 (janitor); 26-27; 28, 30, 31, 32-33, 36-37, 40 (Slimer) & 44; Tecmo-pg 43 (bottom); University of Toronto-pg 23 (theatre); Warner Bros-pg 39 (top) & 43 (top); Wikimedia-pgs 14-15 & 38 (bottom left); William Mumler-pg 18 (bottom).

LIBRARY OF CONGRESS CONTROL NUMBER: 2020948213
PUBLISHER'S CATALOGING-IN-PUBLICATION DATA

Names: Hamilton, S.L., author.

Title: The world's most ghoulish ghosts / by S.L. Hamilton

Description: Minneapolis, Minnesota : Abdo Publishing, 2022 | Series: Xtreme screams | Includes online resources and index.

Identifiers: ISBN 9781532194863 (lib. bdg.) | ISBN 9781644946244 (pbk.) | ISBN 9781098215170 (ebook)

Subjects: LCSH: Ghosts--Juvenile literature. | Ghosts in popular culture--Juvenile literature. | Ghost stories--Juvenile literature. | Ghosts in motion pictures--Juvenile literature. | Ghost television programs--Juvenile literature. | Monsters--Juvenile literature.

Classification: DDC 398.2454--dc23

TABLE OF
Contents

CHAPTER 1
THE WORLD'S MOST GHOULISH
Ghosts

Ghosts are said to be the spirits of people who have died. Some are believed to be good. Some are thought to be evil. Their shape may be a shadowy form of their living selves or nearly invisible **presences**. Are they real or just human **imagination**?

XTREME FACT

A poltergeist is a ghost who makes noise and likes to make its presence known. "Poltergeist" comes from the German words for "knock" and "spirit."

CHAPTER 2

History

A Japanese story tells of a princess who summons a skeleton ghost to terrify soldiers who have come to harm her.

Ghost stories have been told from all cultures around the world. Ghosts are said to haunt everything from homes and businesses to gardens, schools, ships, and battlefields.

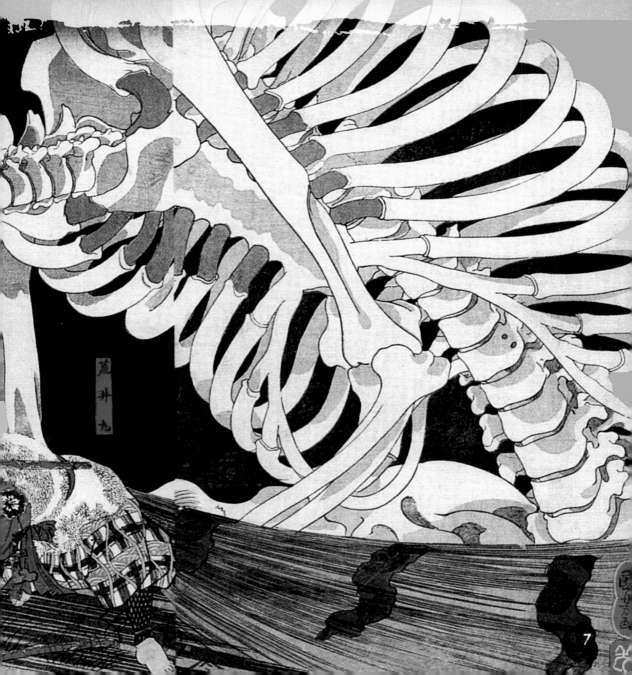

CHAPTER 3
BECOMING A
Ghost

Some believe that ghosts are people with unfinished business in the living world. Did they have a task to do? Information to give loved ones? Or are spirits here because they wish to haunt someone?

Some think that ghosts haunt the living because their lives ended too soon. They may have fallen, drowned, or been in a car accident.

Other spirits are thought to stay because their lives ended violently. Perhaps they were murdered or maybe they took their own life. Whatever the cause, believers think that spirits either choose to stay or are unable to leave the **Earthly realm**.

CHAPTER 4
Famous Mediums

Mediums are people who claim to be able to contact the spirit world. Margaret and Kate Fox were only 12 and 10 years old when they became famous mediums in 1848. They snapped their fingers and a ghost seemed to repeat the sound. Their older sister Leah scheduled their **séances,** and the Fox sisters became wealthy.

XTREME FACT

In 1888, Margaret Fox gave a lecture and showed that the Fox sisters' skills were a hoax. They could snap their big toe joint to sound like a spirit tapping. For decades, their skills seemed real.

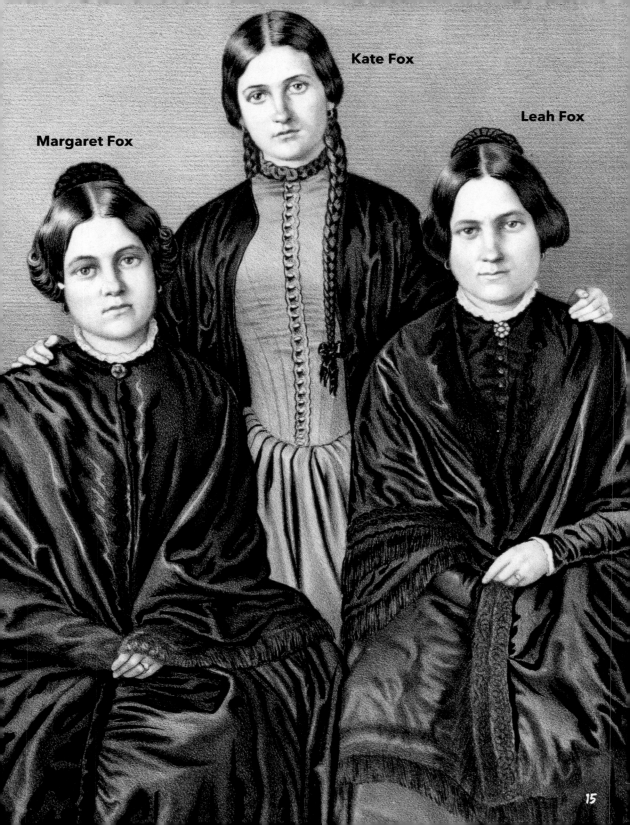

Margaret Fox

Kate Fox

Leah Fox

Modern mediums are seen on television, such as New York's Theresa Caputo and John Edward, and Georgia's Chip Coffey. They attempt to contact family and friends who have died.

Theresa Caputo, *Long Island Medium*

John Edward, *Crossing Over with John Edward*

Chip Coffey, *Paranormal State, Psychic Kids, Kindred Spirits*

XTREME FACT

James Randi was known as the Amazing Randi. The famous magician believed mediums used tricks to make it look like they have paranormal powers.

CHAPTER 5
Ghost Sightings

Homes seem to be popular haunting places. Lady Dorothy Walpole, or The Brown Lady, has been seen in her home in England's Raynham Hall. The White House is said to have ghosts of President Abraham Lincoln and his 11-year-old son, Willie.

A photo from Raynham Hall seems to show a ghostly lady dressed in brown.

Spirit Abraham and Mary Todd Lincoln

XTREME FACT

In the late 1800s, spirit photographs were created by combining an image of a living person and a ghostly image of a dead loved one.

Original owners Thomas and Anna Whaley haunt their home in San Diego, California. The Whaley House is said to be the most haunted house in the United States.

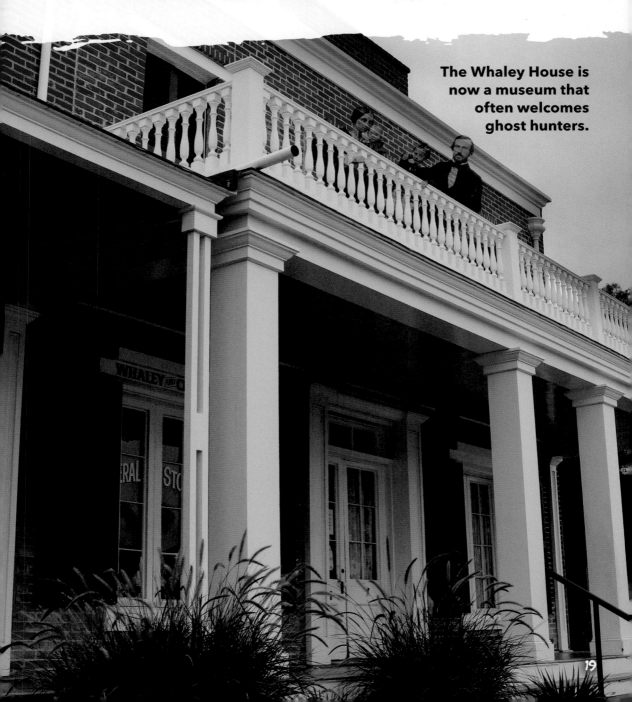

The Whaley House is now a museum that often welcomes ghost hunters.

When William Winchester died in 1881, he left his widow Sarah with his rifle company—and a curse. A medium warned her that she must build an ever-expanding home for the spirits of people killed by Winchester rifles.

Sarah Winchester's San Jose, California, home is open for tours. Some think she haunts it.

The Winchester Mystery House was under construction for 38 years. When Sarah died in 1922, it had 160 rooms, maze-like hallways, doors that opened to empty space, and stairs that led to nowhere.

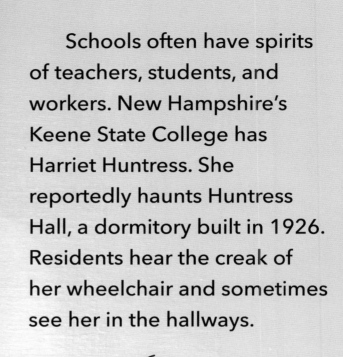

Schools often have spirits of teachers, students, and workers. New Hampshire's Keene State College has Harriet Huntress. She reportedly haunts Huntress Hall, a dormitory built in 1926. Residents hear the creak of her wheelchair and sometimes see her in the hallways.

Some students think Harriet's spirit is checking on them in Huntress Hall.

Huntress Hall

Canada's University of Toronto is fond of Burt, the deceased caretaker of the school's theater. His busy ghost is sometimes seen at work in his blue uniform, often hovering in the theater lobby.

Ghostly Burt is credited with stopping a fire from spreading by alerting the Hart House Theatre's managing director, who was in his office.

XTREME FACT

Some people believe ghosts haunt the location of their death.

23

Cemeteries are natural places to find ghosts. Boxing legend Rocky Marciano and his wife Barbara haunt Florida's Forest Lawn Memorial Gardens.

MARCIANO

ROCKY
1923 — 1969

BARBARA
1928 — 1974

Easton, Connecticut's Union Cemetery may be the most haunted cemetery in America. The White Lady ghost is often seen there.

XTREME FACT

Some people believe ghosts haunt cemeteries because of things that happened after their deaths. Perhaps personal items were stolen from them, or they have no grave marker, or their family moved away.

Ghosts seem to haunt ships. The ocean liner *Queen Mary* is now a hotel and restaurant docked in Long Beach, California. The ghost of a crewman crushed by watertight door #13 has been spotted below decks. The first-class swimming pool also sports ghostly activity with wet footprints, children's voices, and splashing noises, even when the pool area is empty.

The *Queen Mary* was once nicknamed "The Grey Ghost." It was painted grey when it was used to transport soldiers during World War II.

Some people believe a former crewman haunts the *Queen Mary*.

Some commercial airlines have stories of ghostly travelers.

Commercial and military airlines have tales of ghostly pilots, passengers, and mechanics. Continental Aircraft #886 reported a woman calling on the intercom phone, "Help me. I'm cold." But all passengers were asleep.

There are stories of ghostly military planes. A phantom World War II Spitfire plane is said to circle the skies over Biggin Hill, England.

Battlefields are often ghost territories. Gettysburg, Pennsylvania, was the site of a famous American Civil War battle. Nearly 8,000 soldiers died in July 1863. Today, people hear strange noises, muffled shouts and screams, and the sounds of faraway cannons.

At Gettysburg, people report seeing glowing orbs and soldiers in ragged uniforms floating over the ground.

The Battle of the Somme took place in France in 1916. Thousands of World War I soldiers died on the battlefield. The first ghost seen was Lord Kitchener, the British secretary of state. He died 5 months earlier, but soldiers saw him on the battlefield. Other ghostly soldiers appeared as well.

Bugle calls, battle sounds, and feelings of dread haunt visitors to the Somme battlefield.

XTREME FACT

One Somme ghost reportedly whispered to a visitor, "We're still here."

CHAPTER 6
GHOST HUNTING
Equipment

Ghost hunters use different kinds of equipment to detect specters. An electromagnetic field (EMF) meter measures a ghost's electrical energy. However, an EMF also measures energy from sources like televisions, appliances, and electrical wires.

An EMF meter can be used indoors or outside.

Temperature sensing equipment include thermometers and thermal scanners that find **cold spots**. Sudden or extreme temperature changes are thought to be signs of a ghost appearing.

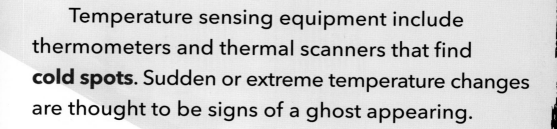

INFRARED THERMOMETER
-50°C - 380°C | 58°F - 716°F

Ghost hunters point an infrared thermometer at a specific place to get a temperature reading.

Other ghost hunting equipment includes motion detectors, cameras, video recording equipment, and **audio recorders**. A thermal imaging scope uses **infrared technology** to see the shape and size of a cold mass detected by a thermal scanner. However, ghost hunters know that their equipment can also detect bugs, animals, and other people.

34

CH1 CH2
CH3 CH4

2015/01/29 18:42:54

PHILIPS

VIDEO PX

BY DIGITAL DOWSING LLC.

Property of
LIPRA

ITC Experimental Device

SLEEP

Panasonic

CHAPTER 7
GETTING RID OF A
Ghost

Getting rid of a ghost may be done with such things as holy water, burning **sage**, and spreading salt around the border of a house. Most **spiritualists** contact the ghost and ask them to leave.

XTREME FACT

The National Association of Realtors say that it is not up to a realtor to tell a buyer about a possible ghost in the house. However, some realtors feel they have a duty to pass on paranormal information.

Those who do not believe in ghosts turn to science to find out what is causing the sounds or **cold spots**. Sometimes even medications can cause people to see things that look like ghosts.

A woman burns sage to cleanse a home of negative energy.

CHAPTER 8
GHOSTS
In the Media

Ghosts are popular characters in millions of books and comic books. **Fictional** ghosts appear and disappear at will, move objects, and may be friends or foes of humans.

Charles Dickens' *A Christmas Carol* **is the 1843 holiday story of the miser Scrooge, who is visited by ghosts with a dire warning.**

The Harry Potter series featured many ghosts. Each of the Hogwarts school's houses had its own ghost: Bloody Baron in Slytherin, Fat Friar in Hufflepuff, Nearly Headless Nick in Gryffindor, and the Grey Lady in Ravenclaw.

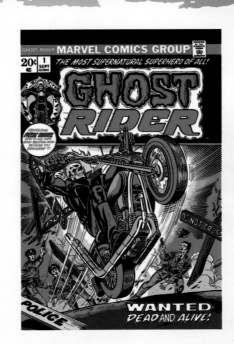

Marvel Comics' *Ghost Rider* is one of many ghost-based comic books. Harvey Comics' Casper, the Friendly Ghost, tried not to scare readers.

Ghosts have become popular effects in movies. They may be funny or they may be terrifying, or both.

Ghostbusters movies have featured both scary and funny ghosts.

Several television shows feature people hunting for ghosts or looking for proof that ghosts exist. Some of the most well-known include *Ghost Hunters*, *Ghost Trackers*, and *Most Haunted*.

Ghost Hunters **starred Jason Hawes and Grant Wilson, researching haunted places.**

In *Most Haunted*, **Yvette Fielding and her team brought viewers to locations that were said to have paranormal activity.**

Ghosts in video games can be helpful or terrifying. Sometimes people play to search and destroy the ghost, and sometimes they play as the ghost.

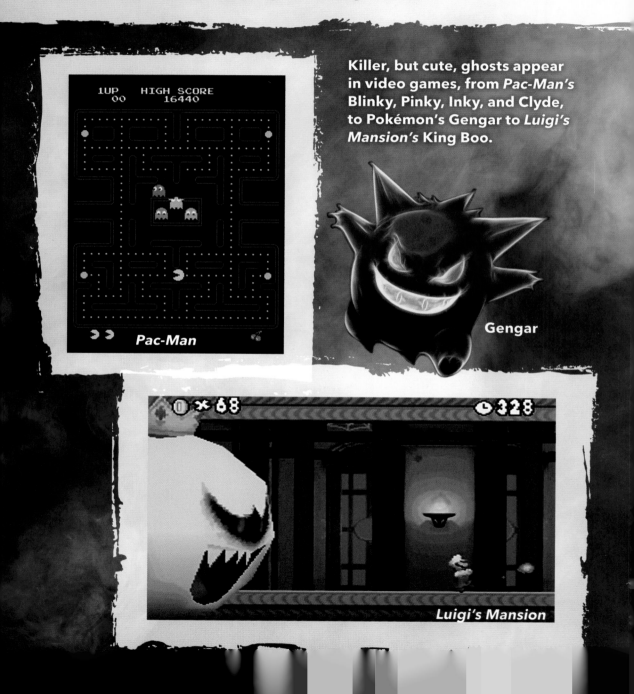

Killer, but cute, ghosts appear in video games, from *Pac-Man's* Blinky, Pinky, Inky, and Clyde, to Pokémon's Gengar to *Luigi's Mansion's* King Boo.

Pac-Man

Gengar

Luigi's Mansion

Middle-earth:
Shadow of Mordor

In *Middle-earth: Shadow of Mordor*, the specter elf lord Celebrimbor has many ghostly powers that he shares with a ranger.

In the *Fatal Frame* games, a player banishes a ghost by using a camera to take the spirit's photo right before it tries to kill.

Fatal Frame 2:
Crimson Butterfly

CHAPTER 9

Are Ghosts Real?

People who do not believe in ghosts look for scientific answers to odd happenings. Others firmly believe that ghosts exist. People decide for themselves.

XTREME FACT

For decades, the James Randi Educational Foundation offered up to $1 million to anyone who could prove the existence of ghosts. No one ever collected the money.

XTREME
Challenge

**TAKE THE QUIZ BELOW AND
PUT WHAT YOU'VE LEARNED TO THE TEST!**

1) What are some common places that ghosts are said to haunt?

2) What do mediums claim they can do? Name two sisters who became famous mediums in the 1800s.

3) What is said to be the most haunted house in the United States?

4) What famous ocean liner is said to be haunted? Where have the ghosts reportedly been seen?

5) List some equipment used by ghost hunters.

6) Some spiritualists say they can get rid of unwanted ghosts. What are some ways they do it?

Glossary

audio recorder – A device that records sounds.

cold spot – A small area where the temperature is colder than the surrounding air. Ghost hunters believe that it is a sign of a spirit. Scientists believe that it is simply drafts or an area that is not close to sunlight or heat.

Earthly realm – Life lived while on Earth. Often used when contrasting what happens to humans after death, when people believe there is an afterlife as a spirit.

fiction – Stories that are made up by a writer or speaker. Not fact.

imagination – To see or create things that are not real, but are formed in a person's mind.

infrared technology – A device that measures infrared radiation. Infrared refers to a certain range of electromagnetic radiation. Visible infrared waves can show variations in temperature, with hotter objects a different color than cooler things.

presence – Being in a certain place.

sage – An herb of grayish-green leaves often used as a flavoring in cooking.

séance – A meeting of a small group of people, led by a medium, to receive spirit communications.

spiritualist – A person who believes that the spirits of dead people can speak to the living, and acts as a go-between to communicate between realms.

Online Resources

Booklinks
NONFICTION NETWORK
FREE! ONLINE NONFICTION RESOURCES

To learn more about the world's most ghoulish ghosts, please visit **abdobooklinks.com** or scan this QR code. These links are routinely monitored and updated to provide the most current information available.

Index